OF CORNWALL

Douglas Williams

BOSSINEY BOOKS

First published in 1987 by
Bossiney Books
St Teath, Bodmin, Cornwall.

Typeset, Printed and Bound by
Clowes Book Printers,
St Columb, Cornwall

To my Mother

Douglas Williams, who has always lived and worked in West Cornwall, has his home at Newlyn, the fishing town where he was born.

Married, with two daughters, he has been a local journalist for over thirty years, and knows West Cornwall, its places and its people, from his own personal involvement in the area, and from his family background here.

Music and drama are among his leisure interests, and he has sung with operatic and choral societies throughout Cornwall. The Rotary Club movement and the Methodist Church also play an important part in his life. A Bard of the Cornish Gorsedd, his Bardic name sums up his interests, 'Voice and Pen'.

In 1984 Douglas Williams made his debut for Bossiney with *Mount's Bay* in which he took readers on a journey – in words and pictures from Land's End to Lizard Light.

Then in 1985 he produced *West Cornwall in the Old Days* which featured stories and photographs that spanned a century. 'The strength of West Cornwall lies in its enchanting variety,' he wrote. 'Every corner and cove, village and stream, harbour and hill, has its power to appeal.'

Now in 1987 he completes a Bossiney hat-trick with *Festivals of Cornwall,* touring some of the great Cornish occasions; Hurling and the Gorsedd, Crying the Neck and Marhamchurch Revel, Flora Day at Helston and Obby Oss at Padstow are only some of the events covered in words and photographs.

'A new spirit of awareness,' he writes, 'is flowering in Cornwall towards its traditional feasts and festivals.

'Through centuries of poverty and rigorous routine the local Gala Days of celebration were anticipated and enjoyed. The fishermen stayed ashore, the farm labourers quit the fields, the miners kept on top.'

The book opens with an introduction to set the scene and is followed by 'A Calendar of Custom' including a month-by-month account of festivals both past and present. As Douglas Williams says, 'It has been impossible to include every event, for most towns and villages celebrate a Carnival, a Feast Day or a Regatta, but this selection illustrates the wealth of tradition and creativity in Cornwall.'

ABOVE **The author receiving the Gorsedd music shield, for services to music in Cornwall, from the Grand Bard, Mr Hugh Miners, in 1985.**

Festivals of Cornwall

ABOVE **The Grand Bard, Richard Jenkin, holding aloft a new trophy at the Gorsedd.**

RIGHT **Fiddler John Care leads the girls at the 1986 John Knill Ceremony in St Ives.**

A new spirit of awareness is flowering in Cornwall towards its traditional feasts and festivals.

Through centuries of poverty and rigorous routine the local Gala Days of celebration were anticipated and enjoyed. The fishermen stayed ashore, the farm labourers quit the fields, the miners kept on top.

These were times of family reunions, religious celebrations, local customs, village fairs and merry-making. Down the years some of the festivities fell into disrepute, others were stopped, many just faded away.

Today, in an age where 'progress' has so many cloaks of change, and precious few are good for Cornwall, its people are slowly appreciating exactly what is at stake.

Week by week, throughout the seasons, from Saltash to Sennen, greater efforts are being made not only to ensure that old customs flourish, but to rally many of those which are in danger of fading, if not of dying out altogether.

What has been particularly encouraging is the role played by those who have come to live in Cornwall, alongside the 'locals', and by those 'exiles' who have returned home in retirement, eager and capable of making a major contribution.

The Federation of Old Cornwall Societies has been a driving force in this revival. Their motto, 'Gather the Fragments that remain, that nothing be Lost', so aptly sums up the spirit of this book. In Cornish it reads *Cuntelleugh an Brewyon Us Gesys Na Vo Kellys Travyth*.

Let us take the festivals by the season, from the joyous springtime of Furry Dance and Hurling matches, to midsummer bonfires and harvest festivals, the autumnal Gorsedd, and then revel in the Cornish carols of Christmas. Around these major festivals are a multitude of others -- carnivals and fairs.

Paradoxically, the creation of six districts in Cornwall, with their takeover of decision-making from the many ancient

boroughs, has kindled a determination in the towns and villages to hold on to their individuality. This, in turn, has brought a renewed interest in their history and traditions.

The days of figgy-pudden, of saffron and heavy cake, of 'ferrins' and home-made pasties are far from over. It is vital, though, to ensure that our genuine festivals are not allowed to degenerate into gimmick-laden entertainments, provided solely for tourist-bait and fund-raising.

Let the Celtic spirit ring through - and true.

It rings out with the Cornish and Celtic festivals around the English-speaking world. The Cousin Jacks have taken this spirit and their songs with them to Australia, Zambia, Canada, South Africa and the United States. When you hear *Camborne Hill* sung ten thousand miles from home you need no further proof!

As Dr Ralph Dunstan pointed out, almost sixty years ago, there is strong reason to believe that Cornwall was an exceptionally musical place during even the eighteenth century. The Wesley revival, and its influence over succeeding generations, crushed

BELOW AND RIGHT The annual Sunday Schools parade and tea treat flourishes even today – particularly here at St Ives. 'Through centuries of poverty the local gala days were anticipated and enjoyed.'

6

many of the secular songs – even if innocent enough – but provided a new heritage with its hymn-singing and our local carols.

Our celebrated male voice choirs and choral societies had their birth and inspiration from the musical training received in the chapels and churches.

The carols of Thomas Merritt are as much a part of our birthright today as the old mine stacks. Music and melody are an integral part of our being, and have a close affinity with all we are, and try to be, within Cornwall.

As well as the happy tunes of Furry Dance and Obby Oss, the Starry Gazey Pie, and dozens more, there are the contrasts with the declamatory national anthem *Trelawny* and the modern and haunting *Boats of Sennen*.

The songs tell of Feast days and working life, of the seasons and special occasions, of elections and regattas, of mermaids and smugglers. Today the youngsters enjoy *Way Down to Lamorna*, and the choirs sing *Hail to the Homeland* with fervour. Malcolm Arnold, Ken Pelmear, Richard Gendall and Goff Richards have made sure that this great musical tradition will continue.

Each year more people are studying and speaking the Cornish language. It is not an esoteric hobby for the eccentric, as some would have us suppose. It plays an increasing, colourful, interesting and important role in our festivals.

It has always done so in the Gorsedd – with 1988 the Diamond Jubilee Year – and in recent years church services in the language have come to the forefront. Harvests and weddings have also been celebrated, and with the great progress in Biblical translation by an expert team has come a new range of opportunities.

Even the banks have agreed to accept cheques made out in Cornish, as they do in some other Celtic nations.

The richness of the dialect, practised so brilliantly and popularly, and the tremendous variety of folklore, help treasure the events of time past. So often the Cornish have relied on writers from outside the county, on their 'visitations', to record our history and customs.

In this century the Cornish have made their own distinguished contributions, from writers of the calibre of Dr A. L. Rowse, Peter Pool, Professor Charles Thomas, Claude Berry, Derek Tangye, Donald Rawe and Cyril Noall. Our poets, such as Charles Causley and Jack Clemo and D. M. Thomas – also famed as a novelist – and

LEFT AND BELOW Carnival remains a lively part of village life, and this Royal group at Gwennap looks very cheerful.

ABOVE Miss Rowena Cade, creator of the Minack Theatre, on her ninetieth birthday.

RIGHT Month in and month out the marathon walkers and runners, pushers and pullers, arrive at Land's End. None did more to popularise the almost 1,000 mile trek from John O'Groats than Dr Barbara Moore. Here I am having an interview with her before her last journey.

our very many fine contemporary artists, add greatly to this twentieth century cultural tapestry.

Yet we cannot fail but be impressed by the crucial part played by those who have come to live here among us, and be grateful to them for their varied gifts.

Though the ignorant may blurt labels of 'emmet' and 'foreigner' I wonder how many will leave the mark of Rowena Cade of Minack, Dame Barbara Hepworth of St Ives, Stanhope Forbes of Newlyn, and the Yglesias sisters of Mousehole? Their love for Cornwall was immense – and it shows.

CAIRO-CORNISH
1939-1945

Were Cornwall ever to catch the attention of those philatelic specialists who choose the postage stamp illustrations, what a selection we could offer! Hurling and Gorsedd, Crying the Neck, the Marhamchurch Revels, the processions for the St Cuthbert Mayne anniversary, the Helston and Padstow celebrations, and the Royal dues presentations are just a few subjects that immediately spring to mind.

The year 1987 was the 650th anniversary of the establishment of the Duchy of Cornwall. In Prince Charles we have a Duke who has been a regular and interested visitor to his lands – perhaps more than any other for 500 years.

The Royal dues ceremony comes only once in a lifetime, but is there an opportunity for a 17 March festival to mark the anniversary of the Duchy Charter? For a festival does not have to be centuries old to have a meaning, and a purpose. Trevithick Day at Camborne, and the new Heritage Day at Bodmin, show what can be developed, inspired by a town tradition, and incorporating the best of the old and new.

It can bring a fresh vitality to a town. I feel sure many others, perhaps through the Old Cornwall Societies, could develop these events, marking great days in their history, and notable personalities, to add further to the character of their area.

We must continue to build on the increasing interest in our heritage, and with a twenty first century approach.

ABOVE Few places outside Cornwall could match this body of 'Exiles' – Cairo Cornish Association (with one lady member) during the war years of 1939–45. 'The Cousin Jacks have taken the Cornish spirit and songs with them around the world.'

Cornwall may be turning more and more rapidly into a holiday park, with its historic industries in decline. Fishing and agricultural quotas, tin mine and factory closures, have put the future of many jobs within Cornwall in jeopardy.

Who knows how long the Herbert Thomas county of 'Pasties and Cream, Tin in the Stream', and of the 'Seven Sorts of Fish' lifestyle, fostered over centuries, will be maintained?

Fundamental changes in our economy may surround and confound us, but the continuity of the Cornish way of life can still flourish. We must ensure that it does.

A Calendar of
Custom

Guise Dancing

TWELFTH NIGHT

The Cornish year has its local landmarks as well as its seasons. Feast days and festivals, whether in winter, autumn, summer, but especially in springtime, bring enormous pleasure. Almost all those I describe in this journey, month by month, through the calendar of custom, continue to thrive.

It is extremely doubtful if New Year's Eve in the old days, was celebrated with the same frantic enthusiasm as we do today. It appears to complete the Christmas festivities, while not so long ago Twelfth Night was the important date. When I was a lad my first experience of 'theatre' came at this time from the last of the gallant 'Geese Dancers'. The second world war, and the 'blackout' put an end to much of this door-to-door entertainment.

It was colourful and a little frightening but, as most of the participants were of stalwart Methodist background, there was little real mischief and no malice. These 'disguised' characters, masked and robed, with faces hidden or blackened, came knocking on the door from Christmas to Twelfth Night.

Hardly up to the mark were those guise dancers in one Cornish town, a hundred years ago or more, who were described as 'a terror to the respectable inhabitants'.

It was a remarkable feature of Cornish life – leading to the death or drastic change of many customs – that 'respectability' was a virtue mightily to be achieved ... at least in appearance. Rowdiness, especially when associated with alcohol, was quietly but firmly stamped out. Notices were posted at Penzance every Christmas Eve, forbidding 'Geese Dancers' in the streets.

In recent years the custom has been revived at St Ives, at Feast in February, rather than Christmas time.

RIGHT AND FAR RIGHT Guise dancers at St Ives Feast today. In earlier days the 'disguised' characters came knocking on the door from Christmas to Twelfth Night.

Hurling
at St Ives

FEAST MONDAY

There was a time when hurling was part of the life of many a Cornish parish. Today the silver ball goes flying in two only, the sands of St Ives on Feast Monday, and the streets and fields of St Columb on Shrove Tuesday and the Saturday of the following week.

Here goes up the Silver Ball,
Free for country, town and all.

This object of so much desire and excitement is about the size of an orange, made of wood or cork, covered by a thin layer of silver.

St Ives Feast takes place on the nearest Sunday to 3 February, and the hurling contest the following morning is between the ancient rivals Uplong and Downlong. The ball is first carried to the holy well of St Ia at Porthmeor, immersed and blessed. The Mayor then stands on the churchyard wall and throws the ball to the waiting players on the sands below with the hurling cry 'Guage Wheg ya guare Teg', Cornish for 'fair play is good play'. It is returned to the Mayor at the Guildhall at noon, and the players, mostly youngsters, are rewarded with coins thrown from the balcony. At one time, I believe, it was a contest between St Ives and Lelant, and then all those called Thomas, William or John competed against everyone else: 'Tom, Wills and Jans take off all's on the sands.'

BELOW AND RIGHT **Flanked by his macebearers, St Ives Mayor J.B. Thomas prepares to throw the Silver Ball to the youngsters on the beach.**

RIGHT The Mayor, J. B. Thomas, is ready to throw the ball to the players on St Ives beach on Feast Monday.

FAR RIGHT Mayor Oakley Eddy throws up the Silver Ball before the start of the contest at St Ives in 1975.

BELOW RIGHT Proudly returning the Silver Ball.

BELOW Mayor Michael Peters throws coins to the youngsters outside the Guildhall on Feast Monday.

Hurling at St Columb

**Shrove Tuesday
and
Saturday of Following Week**

At St Columb the traditional 'Town and Country' duel is a more physically vigorous and adult struggle, with scrum and wrestle.

The Hurlers, standing stones at Minions, St Cleer, in their Druidic Circle, demonstrate what happens to those who profane the Lord's Day by throwing a ball!

Carew in his 1602 *Survey of Cornwall*, described it thus: 'When the hurling is ended, you shall see them retiring home, as from a pitched battle, with bloody pates, bones broken, and out of joint, and sick bruises as serve to shorten their days.'

The cry still goes up at St Columb today:

> *Town and Country do your best*
> *For in this Parish I must rest.*

Shopkeepers and householders take the precaution of

barricading their windows, and at 4.30 p.m. the game begins from the Market Square through the main and side streets. Townmen and countrymen each have their goal – two miles apart – and at 8 p.m. comes the final calling-up of the ball by the winner of the day's hurl. 'Countryman' Michael Weldhen holds the record number of wins. Local historian Ivan Rabey tells me that a remarkable feature of the game over the years is that it 'simply just happens'. 'There is no organising committee, the game does not need one, and the very fact that there is none probably makes for its continued success.'

Shrove Tuesday is also a time for pancakes, ever-popular. In the old times it was a day for cock fighting, and one still hears of the 'tricks' being played, with signs taken down, boats lifted up, and gates unhung!

RIGHT A strenuous St Columb struggle in the 'cloth cap' days of the 1920's.

BELOW Another earlier view of the game. The ball is aloft and the hurling is under way.

St Piran's Day
5 MARCH
and
Esethvos Kernow

As the Gorsedd is the 'bridge' between Cornish cultures so the Eisteddfed or Esethvos Kernow is the 'display cabinet'. It provides, every few years, the opportunity to practise together the arts, whether music or poetry, dance or drama. When last held in 1986 it brought together the Cornish music and drama festivals, youth orchestra, brass bands, Townswomen's Guilds and Women's Institutes, and the Federation of Old Cornwall Societies ... and so many more.

It also linked with another Cornish festival, now revived in interest, St Piran's Day, on 5 March, with processions, banners and a church service.

Legend tells us that this Patron Saint of Cornish Tinners who sailed across the Irish Sea on a millstone, discovered tin smelting, and enjoyed a drink or two. 'As drunk as a Piraner' is an old Cornish proverb! In the old days it was a miners' holiday, and today his emblem of white cross on black background – tin against rock - has become adopted as the 'national' flag.

Bedhens Kernow en Kessenyans
Let Cornwall be in Concord.

Cornwall Music Festival
FIRST WEEK IN MARCH

There was a time in 1972 when it was felt that the Cornwall Music Festival might be fading away, but today it is more healthy and dynamic than ever. The leadership of chairman Dr Edward Weymouth with secretary Ronald Grubb has given it a new vitality. The week-long programme is stronger, with increasing support, particularly from the schools.

Lady Mary Trefusis was its founder, and accompanist, in 1910, and for over sixty years it travelled through Cornwall from Launceston to Penzance. Those indomitable sisters, Maisie and Evelyn Radford, with Sheila Henderson, were at the helm for many years, and brought to the county distinguished musicians such as Sir Adrian Boult, and many fine vocalists.

Herbert Howells, Eric Thiman, Walford Davies, Hugh Robertson and Douglas Guest have been among the adjudicators at a festival which, in recent years, has been centred on Truro's St Clement Methodist Church, during the first week in March.

Covering so many aspects of music-making – the piano accordion is the latest instrument to be included – it has had such competitors, in their youth, as Sir David Willcocks as pianist, and singers Ben Luxon, Alan Opie and Wendy Eathorne.

Our future singers and players have a fine platform for their young talents, for the festival covers all aspects of amateur music in the county and is closely linked to the Gorsedd.

Music Making

Music-making has never been of such high calibre in Cornwall as today, from the East Cornwall Bach Festival to the Penzance Orchestral Society which celebrated its eightieth birthday in 1986.

Another major event is the comparatively recent Three Spires Festival, at Truro, in 1987 to be held in June. The sterling work of Albert and Betty Sinfield contributed to its success and to that of the earlier Mylor Festival. For Cornwall is now ringing with music of the highest standard throughout the seasons, from St Endellion to St Buryan.

The great West of England band festival at Bugle, the Cornwall male voice choir open championships at St Austell close to the Spring Bank Holiday, and the prestigious International Musicians Seminar, led by Sandor Vegh, are three contrasting and exciting attractions.

Duchy Opera, and the many amateur operatic societies, the Kenwin Barton Gilbert and Sullivan Society at Truro, and the choral societies that span the county all contribute to a massive resurgence of song. They join the long-established male voice choirs that have given Cornwall a great reputation.

Nowadays the Cornish male choirs have an international audience, with Transatlantic visits, and many trips to France and Germany.

ABOVE **The scene at St Austell with the Cornwall open male voice championships. Here conductor George Smith is seen with the winners Holman Climax choir.**

BELOW This Copper Shield is still a leading trophy at the Cornwall music festival. It was made of Cornish copper at St Ives to a design by the founder Lady Mary Trefusis. The other trophies are those previously awarded, including a cup for school choirs, male voice quartets, and the banner at the back for sight singing...perhaps a lost art in schools these days.

West Cornwall Spring Show

MID MARCH

Spring comes earlier in West Cornwall – as a successful group has been proving for over sixty years.

Way back in 1922 a few professional growers put on a show of their produce at Ridgeovean farm cartshed at Gulval on a Friday afternoon. From this humble start came the Western Commercial Spring Show, which had its first official show the following year, and 'It is still thriving' so Charles Tregoning, a member of that original committee, and a former president, tells me.

Those two giants in Cornish horticulture, H.W. Abbiss and Alec Gray, were to the forefront of its development, with the aim of putting the early Cornish produce, mainly daffodils and cauliflowers, 'on the map' nationally.

The West Cornwall Spring Show is held at St John's Hall, Penzance, in Mid-March, with the professional accent still strong and regarded as very important for the industry. The displays always make a glorious sight, with an impressive range of locally bred varieties of flowers and plants on view. There is a wide interest for the general public with the popular flower arranging, and the Women's Institutes' and Schools' sections.

BELOW A St Ives tradition is model boat sailing at the Consols Pool on Good Friday.

Villagers in an old tradition, now almost forgotten, went to St Nant's – sometimes called the Lady Nance – holy well on Palm Sunday, at Little Colan, near Newquay, and dropped palm crosses in the water. If a cross sank, its owner could expect an early death!

Good Friday in Cornwall is notable for its annual musical programmes, such as the oratorio performance at Camborne Wesley Church, but there are other traditions. At the Consols Pool at St Ives there is small-boat sailing during the morning. Throughout the day hundreds complete the walk by cliffpath and road 'away down to Lamorna'.

Top soccer attraction on Easter Monday for 100 years has been the final of the Cornwall Senior Cup, won for three recent years in a row, 1984–6, by Liskeard. This is a double-feature event, once with the runners-up play-off, but now with the Junior Cup final, won by Fowey in '86. The occasion generates great interest, and for many years was played on the St Austell ground, but nowadays is shared around the county, with Newquay, Bodmin and Truro getting their chance.

Cornwall Garden Society Spring Flower Show

With Prince Charles as its Patron, the Cornwall Garden Society had a special celebration in 1987 with its seventy-fifth Spring Flower show.

Almost always held in April, and usually staged at the Truro City Hall, it went 'under canvas' at the Trelissick Estate for its major anniversary events.

It is regarded as the largest show of its kind in the South West of England, was visited by the Queen Mother in 1981, and aims 'to foster the love of gardens and gardening', as general secretary Dr Challinor Davies explained.

The society, by various names, has run unbroken since 1897, but two world wars brought a break in the annual displays. The president is David Trehane and chairman Lady Falmouth. The society continues to show Cornwall at its loveliest.

Trevithick Day

LAST SATURDAY IN APRIL

There is still a Richard Trevithick in Cornwall, and he is the great-great-great-great-great grandson of that great engineer! He is proud, as so many are, of the work being done to mark Trevithick Day at Camborne. Rightly so, for it has grown to become one of the county's newest and biggest celebrations.

The contemporary Richard, of Callington, would like to see a 'gathering of the clan' some day, and such a world-wide Trevithick re-union would make a marvellous highlight.

RIGHT The centenary of the death of Richard Trevithick was marked at Camborne in 1933 in paying tribute to the town's greatest son.

BELOW A contemporary Trevithick Day scene with dancers parading past the statue.

The last Saturday in April is the big day – Trevithick was born in this month and died in April 1833 – with his statue gazing down on the lively parade. He was the 'father of the locomotive' and inventor of the screw propellor.

'It is a celebration of Camborne's involvement with the Industrial Revolution,' said chairman Trevor Dalley. 'He was born at Pool, is our most famous son, and we have a new theme each year about his life or Camborne's history. There has been overwhelming support.' Thousands of pounds have been raised for charities and the processions have included traction engines and bands, dancers, vintage cars, choirs and hundreds of children, as well as a host of stalls and displays.

ABOVE **What would Trevithick Day be without the traction engine?**

MAY

May Day
at
Padstow

**If 1 May is on a Sunday it is
held on the Monday.**

A celebration with a local colour all its own is May Day and the Obby Oss at Padstow.

Those who love the song and the dance, the uninhibited and energetic fun, and infectious merriment, who treasure the traditions of the townsfolk, savour these hours. Some believe it had its origin in the fourteenth century when a French landing party mistook red-coated mummers for soldiers, and fled. Others think that the French mistook the Oss, on guard at Stepper Point, as 'the evil one'.

The only way to capture its atmosphere is to be there. Words, photographs and film fail to portray fully the physical excitement and relish of this unique welcome to summer.

Unite and Unite, and let us all unite
For Summer is acome unto day,
And whither we are going we will all unite
In the merry morning of May.

The Blue Ribbon 'Peace' Oss, introduced after the first world war, is first to make its appearance, at 10 a.m., from the Institute, followed by the Old 'Red' Oss – as always from the Golden Lion – an hour later. The insistent and hypnotic beat of the drum, the

BELOW The Blue Ribbon Oss dances through the streets of Padstow on May Day in 1962.

FAR RIGHT The accordions and the drums and the traditional dress in the flag-decked streets in the 1970s

ABOVE **Memories of the old times at Padstow are revived by this photograph.**

RIGHT **The excitement mounts among the crowd in the narrow street.**

singing and the music of the accordions, the 'Teazing' of the Oss make up the pattern, with the two meeting around the Maypole for a dance in the evening.

'Nowhere else is found such a powerful May Song, nowhere else such a vigorous, if at times terrifying, hobby horse,' writes Donald Rawe, a Padstonian and Cornish Bard.

The characters and decorations, the paraders, the thrill of seeing the Oss for the first time, the allegiance of Red and Blue, and the family ties and loyalties, all contribute to the richness of a May Day tradition so clearly cherished. It was summed up over 150 years ago in this way: 'The bones of every Padstow boy are fired by the Hobbyhorse. As soon as a child is able to lisp its parents name, it will chant the glorious strains of our ancient festival Song.'

May Day

1 MAY

LEFT It is the golden jubilee of Biscovey School at Par, in 1962.

BELOW It is Empire Day in 1906 and the children of St Paul's School at Penzance entertain at the Recreation Ground.

You may not always see children, dressed in white, dance around the Maypole at Lanreath on May Day, but you could well see the tall pole in place. That is – if it hasn't been stolen! For this village, a half-mile off the road between Middle Taphouse and Looe, has an unusual and distinctive tradition, as Mrs Lila Facey of the Farm and Folk Museum told me.

Towards the end of April a group of local youngsters get together, decide to erect a pole, and – more recently – place it in a field at the back of Lanreath. Previously it was in front of the parish church. It is often 80-90 feet high, and in the 1970s a record was set for the highest Maypole in the country, over 100 feet. So begins the competition, for at this stage the rivals of nearby Pelynt, Lerryn, and Dobwalls try to take it away.

The local youngsters keep guard, and if they can retain it for a month the pole will be cut up into a set of skittles. The pole in 1986, though, was in a rather poor state at the end of the duel! 'It can get to quite a rough house, with plenty of excitement,' said Mrs Facey who has a 'wood' for the skittles, made from an old Maypole, in the museum which she runs with husband, John, and family. Tug-of-war competitions are also part of the celebrations.

BELOW Maypole dancing at St Ives Junior School.

LEFT **May Day at Lanreath in the 1950s,** with a traditional scene outside the church.

Flora Day

8 MAY
**If this should fall on a
Sunday or Monday, then it is
held on the preceding Saturday**

Some Cornish festivities retain their individualism from their impromptu spirit. Helston Flora Day and the Furry Dance, on 8 May, are enjoyed with style, dignity and charm derived both from its discipline and organisation as well as its natural beauty.

Exiles remember their visits 'Home for Flora' for the rest of their lives. The town band breaking into the familiar strains of the famous melody after the stroke of 12-noon at the Guildhall has a magic of its own.

Some 1,500 dance during the day, for there are also the Early Morning, Children's and the 5 p.m. dances. Make sure to get to Helston early, for the costumes and the revels of the Hal-an-Tow – with St George and the Dragon – set the day off with a smile.

Summer is a Come-O
And winter is a Gone-O

This is the Feast of Archangel St Michael, the town is bedecked with greenery, lily-of-the-valley, and with happiness. Even the figures in the stained glass window at the church take part in the dance! Up to 40,000 people crowd the town. The participation and

BELOW **The children dance at Helston in the 1970s.**

FAR RIGHT **Turn back the clock for this Children's Dance in 1950.**

ABOVE A unique Flora Day in 1910. Because of the death of King Edward VII it was held in July – and the weather was cold!

FAR RIGHT In and out of the Houses – with the black toppers in 1950.

pleasure is stronger than ever, for there were times in the past century when the custom faded. The devoted service of the late Edward Cunnack, who came to be known as 'Mr Flora Day' did much to establish its present reputation, and this faithful work continues.

The first dance through the town at 7 a.m. and then the colourful Hal-an-Tow, get the celebrations under way, and all find the Children's dance at 10.30 a.m. of special appeal.

Nothing, however, holds the attention more – as the people crowd around the Guildhall – than that wait during the final minute to Mid-day. The clock strikes, the band begins to play, and the dancers emerge into an exciting blend of theatre and history. The leaders of this dance must be 'Helston Born', and to them goes a great honour.

They really all do go 'in and out of the houses', as I discovered when I took part during the 1950s, and they travel along the traditional route, to rest in the gardens of Lismore, before completing the circle of the town.

Over 150 years ago many towns in Cornwall danced the Flora:

Falmouth and Truro, Penzance, St Mawes and Saltash among them.

The stranger to Helston, though, should make quite sure of the date. If 8 May falls on a Sunday or Monday the festivities usually take place on the preceding Saturday. In 1910, because of the death of Edward VII it was postponed to mid-July, and in 1886 was cancelled because of the deaths of two leading townspeople.

Today grey top hats have replaced black silk toppers for the men in morning suits, but all eyes are on the ladies in their picture hats and beautiful dresses. In an out of the houses they all dance, sometimes like a long multi-hued serpent down the streets, sometimes in a clockwork spiral – and always smiling.

ABOVE AND RIGHT **The Mid–day dancers, beautifully dressed, enjoy the day.**

FAR RIGHT **The Hal–an–Tow by the Grylls Memorial at Helston, with St George getting the better of things.**

One of the most delightful parts of the St Ives Mayor-making, held on the third Monday in May, is the customary drinking from the silver Loving Cup, which was presented to the Corporation in 1640 by Sir Francis Bassett of Tehidy. The inscription tells all:

> *If any discord twixt my friends arise*
> *Within the Borough of Beloved St Ives*
> *It is desired that this my cup of Love*
> *To every one a peacemaker may prove,*
> *Then I am blest to have given a legacy*
> *So like my heart unto Posterity.*

This beautiful trophy, 33 inches high to the top of the head of the armoured figure, is displayed at the Guildhall. The school children drink from it when they meet the new Mayor and Mayoress, and it is also used by distinguished guests on special occasions.

Mayor Making at St Ives

THIRD MONDAY IN MAY

During John Wesley's fourth visit to Cornwall, in July 1745, he declared: 'I never remember so great an awakening in Cornwall, wrought in so short a time, among young and old, rich and poor, from Trewint quite to the sea shore.'

Trewint, then and now, has a treasured place in the tradition, and each year, on 24 May, a Wesley Day service takes place at this village, near Altarnun.

The link was forged when two travelling preachers, John Nelson and John Downes, arrived tired and hungry at the home of Digory and Elizabeth Isbell, and were given food and shelter. 'Let us go to yonder house, where the stone porch is, and ask for something,' said Nelson. 'We have bread, butter and milk, and good hay for your horse,' said Elizabeth. The preachers stayed – and prayed – and preached. Digory added two rooms to his cottage, and Wesley himself made six visits here, baptized one of the Isbell babies, and conducted open-air services from the stone porch. Digory remarked: 'I have read somewhere in the Bible how that some have entertained angels unawares.' They were the first who entertained the Methodist preacher in Cornwall.

Down the years the Trewint rooms, known locally as Jack's House, fell into disuse and eventually became a roofless ruin, but in

Wesley Day at Trewint

24 MAY

FAR LEFT   The St Ives Loving Cup with former Mayor, Mr Terry Tonkin, giving a school boy a helping hand.

ABOVE An artist's impression of John Wesley preaching from the stone porch at Trewint.

FAR RIGHT The stone porch today at Wesley Cottage, Trewint, where an annual service is held.

1948 were bought for £50 and almost £1,500 spent on restoration. The cottage re-opened on 24 May – the date of Wesley's conversion – in 1950, and the service has continued on that anniversary. Stanley Sowton was the leading spirit in the restoration, and the present secretary of the Methodist Trust, Lionel Rogers, tells me that Sunday afternoon services take place during the summer, led by local youth groups. Almost 250 years after the first visit the rooms have become a place of pilgrimage for thousands.

Over the door of the old chapel at nearby Altarnun is a half-relief stone sculpture (1836) of the head of John Wesley, by Nevil Northey Burnard, who was related to the Isbells of Trewint.

Annual Methodist Service at Gwennap Pit

Spring Bank Holiday Monday

John Wesley preached eighteen times in Gwennap Pit, and this great Methodist tradition continues year by year. His first visit was in 1762, his last in 1789, and he called it 'my amphitheatre' with its 'tiers of people'.

In 1806, so Methodist historian the Reverend Tom Shaw informs me, it was remodelled, making it smaller, but more even. The 'Pit' that Wesley knew was oval – the falling in of old mine workings – and it became a circle about three-quarters the size of the original.

There has been an annual service here since 1807, until recently on Whit Monday, with the famous preachers of Methodism among its guests. There was a festive attraction also with the annual holiday fair at nearby Redruth! Today the service is held on Spring Bank Holiday Monday, but far from the 32,000 mentioned by Wesley, a thousand people will fill it. There were 700 present in 1986, and nowadays the Pit is also used for other purposes, musical and dramatic.

In 1986 the Wesley Panels were placed at the approach, featuring his message 'O Let me Commend my Saviour to You', and illustrated by mosaic and sculptured figures, to show the spread of Methodism and the history of this preaching place.

Just one and a half miles away is the museum of the Cornish Methodist historical association, at Carharrack, with its story of the Wesley visits, Victorian Methodism and other events of the church in the county.

ABOVE **Bowlers and boaters at Gwennap Pit in 1898.**

Hilarity and mockery combined in the election of Mock Mayors. The civic leaders and their retinue came in for some hearty abuse from these costumed characters, during the Feast week celebrations.

At Polperro the 'Mayor' was dipped into the sea, at Penryn he was carried in a chair, preceded by torchbearers and two town sergeants in gowns and cocked hats.

Helston and St Buryan joined in the fun, and there was even a Mayor of Mylor! Sometimes he rode with sceptre, sword and crown, there was usually plenty of ale, good food, and parading. At Lostwithiel a century ago the torchlight procession was watched by 1,000.

Mock Mayors

BELOW There is always hilarity when a 'Mock Mayor' takes over and in 1932 these men of Madron marked the likely extension of the old borough of Penzance with due solemnity!

Minack
Theatre

May to Mid September

RIGHT Miss Rowena Cade, creator of the Minack Theatre, on her ninetieth birthday.

FAR RIGHT The cliffside Minack Theatre during a presentation by Shiva Theatre of Amadeus in 1986.

What was a garden on the Porthcurno cliffs has become one of Britain's most magical theatres. From the first amateur production in 1932 – it was Shakespeare's *The Tempest* – to the present full season of music and drama, with comedy, classics and light opera, the Minack Theatre has grown in reputation and appeal.

Tens of thousands make their way to this open-air auditorium hewn out of the rocks by Miss Rowena Cade and her helpers. It was once the bottom of the gulley next to a cliff garden. The granite outcrops became the wings, and the rows of seats were cut and shaped.

Once the stage was of turf, there were no facilities for the players 'back-stage' -- behind there was a drop to the sea -- and no lighting console to augment the moonlight! Today there are modern amenities, and many improvements, but still the audience has to take its chance with the Cornish weather.

Theatre companies travel from many parts of the country to enjoy a week's production here, and the rare experience of performing in such a marvellous environment. No stage can have such a backcloth of sand and sky, sea and shore, with the richness of the sunlight by day and the darkening hues by night.

There is now a sixteen-week season, beginning at the end of May and continuing to mid-September. In 1986 well over 40,000 watched the productions.

JUNE
Royal Cornwall Show

EARLY JUNE

It really is the 'Royal' Cornwall Show. Monarchs, Princes and Princesses have graced this event down the years. There have been over 150 shows since the Royal Charter was granted in 1827, but its origin goes further back to the original Cornwall Agricultural Society in 1793.

From 1858 it was 'on the move' from town to different town for a century, but in 1960 it settled at Wadebridge, and has grown enormously in size, stature and popularity.

For the past thirty years Albert Riddle has been secretary, and helped its rise to one of the most financially successful in the country. In 1986 there was a record attendance of 105,348. Back in 1886 at St Austell, over two days, the total was just 16,551.

It acts 'as a sounding board for opinions and controversies on the state of agriculture' in the county. Not everyone, however, appreciates the vast amount of preparation that goes into the present three-day show, held on a Thursday, Friday and Saturday in early June. Hundreds work hard to make it an annual triumph.

The future looks bright, for a quarter of those who attend are under twenty years of age, and 12,000 children pay for admission.

Agriculture is Cornwall's No 1 business. Livestock and professional husbandry lie at the heart of this Royal show, but it aims to appeal to all town and country people, with a great range of interest and entertainment.

RIGHT **Members of the Royal family have been frequent visitors to the Royal Cornwall Show. The Queen Mother – then Queen Elizabeth – with Princess Margaret, arrives at the Women's Institute tent at the show in Callington in July 1950.**

ABOVE The St John Ambulance flag dips in salute for the Queen on her Jubilee visit to the Royal Cornwall showground at Wadebridge in August 1977 where many uniformed organisations and young people greeted her.

LEFT The Prince of Wales, later to become Duke of Windsor, pictured with the Scouts.

ABOVE Country events continue throughout the summer and the steam rollers are
always a popular sight.

RIGHT Bird shows still flourish – like this
one at Penzance early this century.

ABOVE Little can match the grandeur and serenity of the horse ploughing team. The annual ploughing matches continue to be a popular part of the farming scene, typified in this 1968 photograph at Roseworthy.

LEFT In the old days an agricultural show could not have a better end than a concert. The Rugby stand at Redruth is packed for the entertainment in 1909.

Bugle
Band Contest
JUNE

RIGHT **Mr Eddie Williams,** musical director of the St Dennis Band, receiving the Royal Trophy – given in 1913 by the then Prince of Wales – from Mr E. H. Grimes in 1961. On the right is Sir Alan Dalton.

What better name than Bugle for a band festival? High amid the china-clay country the harmonies ring out. For 75 years the West of England Bandsmen's Festival, more popularly known as the Bugle band contest, has flourished. It is the only outdoor band contest held in the United Kingdom, and this unique atmosphere brings a social and friendly dimension to the whole occasion.

Perhaps it is best summed up by a man who led St Dennis to the championship trophy every year from 1962-71, the late Eddie Williams. 'The assembly, the march down the field, the dash off to rehearse, the waiting, all are part of the scene, but to me "Bugle" is where old friendships are renewed – created over the years of competition, and re-lived on the day.'

Held in June each year, at the Molinnis Park soccer ground, it caters not only for the senior bands, but there are four graded sections – including youth. Camborne town band has featured many times among the top honours. Forty-two trophies are competed for, a magnificent display.

'The contest has done a great deal to improve the standards of brass bands in Cornwall, and without it many bands would not have progressed into national championship class,' comments president John Skelton. Young people take a great interest in brass banding, so the outlook is most encouraging.

ABOVE **No village was complete without its band. Here are the Newbridge music-makers.**

FAR RIGHT **The conductor complete with beard, and members of the Illogan reed and brass band.**

An important contribution has been made to Cornish life by its composers, conductors and bandsmen. 1986 brought a large increase in entries, and every effort is being made to 'move with changing times' while retaining traditions. One of these is the march to the village centre after the adjudication, where thousands gather to hear the championship winners close the day with a well-loved hymn tune.

LEFT Bands have always been in demand for festivals and ceremonies. Here the deeds of the ships and the men of the Falmouth Packet Boat service are remembered on the Moor by this granite obelisk. The dedication ceremony, pictured here, was in November 1898, with a parade led by the band of HMS Ganges.

ST CUTHBERT MAYNE
Annual Pilgrimage at Launceston

Second or Third Sunday in June

When Father Michael Howard was a student in Rome in 1970 he was present at the Canonisation ceremony at St Peter's for Cornwall's own Saint Cuthbert Mayne.

'Little did I ever think that I should be parish priest at Launceston, and take part in the annual pilgrimage,' he told me.

Cuthbert Mayne's martyrdom is remembered each June, close to the scene and anniversary of his death in 1577, by a procession to the Castle Green, where an open-air Mass is held. He had been ministering to the staunch local Catholics, was arrested and tried, dragged through the streets, and hanged, drawn and quartered. Mayne who was living at Golden Manor, had with him a Papal Bull, announcing the Holy Year of 1575, and an Agnus Dei medal around his neck. These items formed the major part of the charges against him.

His head was stuck over the Castle Gate, but was later taken away and hidden. The skull is borne annually on a 'glass-domed flower-bedecked bier by his fellow Catholics', writes local historian Arthur Venning. It is carried to the town from Lanherne Convent, and the mark of the sixteenth century pike is still plainly visible.

The pilgrimage takes place on the second or third Sunday in June with many joining in the procession from the Guildhall.

ABOVE LEFT **A procession during Pilgrimage Day in the 1930s at Launceston to mark the martyrdom of Saint Cuthbert Mayne.**

ABOVE **Cardinal Griffin speaks during his visit to Launceston and the pilgrimage in 1952.**

Midsummer Eve Bonfires

23 JUNE

BELOW It is Midsummer Eve, June 1961, on St Breoke Down and the Lady of the Flowers, Angela Toms, throws her bouquet into the flames.

FAR RIGHT Mayor Michael Peters lights the Midsummer Bonfire at St Ives.

Midsummer Eve, 23 June, means bonfire night for quite a few thousand – when Cornwall gets 'lit up'. These make a respectable contrast to the old nights of blazing tar barrels through the towns, a hazardous pursuit. And they have developed from the times when villagers linked hands and danced around the fires to preserve themselves from witchcraft.

The Old Cornwall Societies have done much to give them a fresh life and pattern, with prayers in Cornish, a sheaf of herbs and wild flowers thrown on to the fire by the Lady of the Flowers - destroying evil and strengthening good – and an explanation of the colourful ceremonies.

The first to be lit is at Chapel Carn Brea near Land's End, and the fiery chain continues to Kit Hill on the Cornish border.

A tablet on the wall of St Keverne churchyard tells a slice of our history in Cornish as well as in English. This is very fitting, for it is in memory of Michael Joseph, the smith, and Thomas Flamank, the 'leaders of the Cornish host who marched to London, and suffered vengeance there' on 27 June in 1497.

On each anniversary of their execution on Tower Hill, members of Mebyon Kernow, who erected the memorial in 1966, place a wreath here. They marched against taxation by Henry VII for the Scottish war, six months before the equally ill-fated Perkin Warbeck rising.

'They shall have a name perpetual and a fame permanent and immortal.'

Anniversary
OF THE EXECUTION OF
Michael Joseph
and
Thomas Flamank

27 JUNE

The colour and splendour of medieval pageantry came to St Michael's Mount on a sunny day in 1977. With Knights of the Order of St John of Jerusalem wearing their robes, and with banners held aloft, the Grand Prior, the Duke of Gloucester, attended a special service in the ancient chapel there.

Looking down on this scene on the battlements, one could have turned the calendar back through the centuries. As Lord St Levan – then Mr John St Aubyn -- commented to me at the time: 'It would be very sad if the Mount became nothing more than a tourist attraction. This is living history to go into the history books, and I think the Benedictine monks would very much approve of it.'

An annual service of re-dedication, with investitures, takes place on a Sunday in June. The reason for the service lies in historic links between the chapel and the Knights Hospitallers, the most ancient order of chivalry in this country, and from whom descended the present Order of St John.

Consent was given for the Great Banner of the Order to be flown at the Mount on appropriate occasions, and for the banner to be hung in the chapel. Lord St Levan was very keen that the ancient links should be re-established, and so, from the first service for members of the Order in Cornwall in 1976, and the visit of the Duke the following year, this spectacular ceremony has continued each summer.

The Duke and his father are among the many Royal visitors to the Mount over the past century or so. Others are Queen Victoria and Prince Albert, King Edward VII and Queen Alexandra when they were Prince and Princess of Wales, the Queen Mother, Princess Margaret, Princess Alexandra and the Duke of Kent.

Annual Service of Knights of the Order of St John

SUNDAY IN JUNE

LEFT **A procession to the chapel of St Michael's Mount for the annual Order of St John service.**

FAR LEFT **The colourful scene inside the Mount chapel.**

BELOW Carnivals and Tea Treats still survive today. Here children and parents pose for a picture at the Redruth United Methodist tea treat in 1915.

ABOVE A carnival float in the old style. Here are the Redruth 'Queen' and her attendants in 1936. Few towns are without their summertime carnival procession.

LEFT Treglown's picnic grounds at Marazion were a popular venue. This was taken in 1905.

Newquay
1900 Week

From First Sunday in July

A new festival that has captured the imagination of thousands of local people and visitors is the Newquay 1900 Week. It starts on the first Sunday in July, and was introduced because this was a 'quiet week' for tourism in the town. 'Now the visitors come especially for it, book in advance, and dress up in costumes of the 1900s with the Newquay people,' said former secretary Neville Hogarth, recently chosen as the resort's first Town Crier for forty years.

So successful was it in 1986, that over 50,000 watched the firework display at the harbour and the torchlight procession through the town on the final Friday night. The cliffs were lined with people.

Shop assistants and hotel workers also dress on this theme, and the programme ranges from a Festival-of-the-Sea service to a beach day, vintage car rally, picnic parties, fashion shows, and a very popular carnival. Hundreds of children take part in the events, and in just five years the committee – with representatives from every organisation in the town – has seen the Week develop into the happiest success story of the year.

Everyone joins in the fun at the Newquay
1900 Week, from the jovial procession
ABOVE LEFT to the Furry Dance ABOVE and
the children at the Maypole LEFT.

Bodmin Riding

**Saturday, 11 July or
Saturday preceding that date**

RIGHT The style and elegance of the
Bodmin Riding in Fore Street.

Although many festivals have vanished with hardly a trace during the past century, one that has been revived to bring a touch of medieval pageantry is the Bodmin Riding, now celebrated with Heritage Day.

It may have had its origin in the fourteenth century, when the Chantry was built, and it culminated with an offering of flowers at the shrine of St Thomas à Becket. The people of Bodmin rode out into the countryside to gather their flowers, returning to the Priory for the presentations, a service and then sports. 'There was also plenty of ale to be drunk,' wrote local historian James Willmott. 'This was one of the reasons why the Riding came to an end, through the impact of Methodism and non-conformist teetotalism in the town.'

The last time the 'Riding' was held on its own was in 1976 – but ten years later was alive again! It returned in a new form, with the whole town, young and old, joining in. 'It was successful beyond our wildest dreams,' said the Mayor, Mrs Christine Beelders.

Street stalls, entertainments, sports, plenty of costumes – and horses and riders – attracted thousands to the town on Saturday 5 July in 1986. The organising committee plan to hold the event regularly on the Saturday on or before 11 July each year.

The 1549 Cornish rebellion against the Prayer Book translation – and defeat – was re-enacted, and so was the civic banquet that ended with Mayor Boyer being hanged on Mount Folly outside the Shire Court. Town Mayors have an easier time of it today!

LEFT Turning the spitted ram for the Mayor's Banquet at the Bodmin Riding.

BELOW The King's Provosts lead the triumphant Royal Army away from the battlefield when they crushed the rebel Cornish Army.

John Knill Ceremony

Every Five Years On 25 JULY

Ten little girls dressed in white and two elderly widows follow where the fiddler leads. Round and around the Knill Steeple they go to the tune of the Cornish Furry Dance. This unique St Ives tradition, begun in 1801, takes place once every five years, with the most recent one being held on St James Day, 25 July 1986.

In 1782, John Knill, one of the town's most celebrated personalities, built the Steeple – a granite mausoleum in the shape of a pyramid fifty feet high – and drew up the details for the ceremony. He was Collector of Customs from 1762-82 and Mayor in 1767, but he was not a native of the town, for he was born in Callington, and his remains do not rest here, but in London.

Knill was present at that first ceremony 185 years ago, and left money for gifts for those taking part, and for a dinner. But some claimed he was in league with the smugglers and that he erected the Steeple as a daymark at this prominent spot! A Customs Officer, the Mayor and the Vicar are Trustees and the monument bears Knill's Coat of Arms, the motto *Resurgam* and the text 'I Know that my Redeemer Liveth'.

John Care has been the fiddler here for over 25 years, succeeding his grandfather in a tradition which he enjoys and – like the whole of St Ives -- believes is well worth continuing.

BELOW AND RIGHT Up the hill at St Ives and on the way to the Knill Steeple.

ABOVE A crowded scene at the Steeple.

RIGHT The Master of Ceremonies, Harding Laity, leads one of the widows in the Knill ceremony.

ABOVE The little girls dance to the music of fiddler John Care.

ABOVE Time for a break at the John Knill ceremony in 1986.

RIGHT The Knill Festival in the old days.

With a membership of 1,200 in 24 clubs from St Buryan, in the west, to Stratton and across to Landrake, the Cornwall Federation of Young Farmers Clubs is in great heart. The annual rally, usually in the last week of July, holds special significance in 1987 with celebrations to mark its Golden Jubilee and the 650th anniversary of the creation of the 'Duchy', led by chairman Richard Jenkin (Launceston).

Mick Alsey, for 24 years the YFC organiser, tells me that some 800 members take part in the rally which is enjoyed by 3,000. After the annual competitions day in May this rally has many entertaining features with its sports events.

There is also the practical side with tractor driving, stock judging and flower arranging, together with displays of cooking, handicraft, art and photography, in a large marquee.

The first rally was way back in 1937 at Pencarrow. 'Young farmers clubs today are not as insular as they were 24 years ago, and do a tremendous amount of work for the community,' he added. They raise between £20,000 - £40,000 a year for various charities.

LEFT Mayor Michael Peters and widow at the Knill Steeple.

ABOVE AND BELOW Huge crowds watch the Regatta at Hayle in 1931 (above) and 1905 (below). Today most harbours still hold their regatta.

ABOVE What a charming summer scene: the piers are packed for the Mousehole harbour sports.

Goldsithney Charter Fair

FIRST SATURDAY IN AUGUST

Even when the annual Goldsithney Charter Fair was not being regularly celebrated, one part of the tradition was retained: a gauntlet hung outside the Trevelyan Arms every 5 August. For, in the old days, gloves were suspended from high poles to signal the opening of the Fair, and were jealously guarded. Perhaps it was part of the 'throwing down the gauntlet' ceremony, as this Fair had its origin some miles away at Sithney, near Helston until – legend tells us – some enterprising character ran off with it. He made for Goldsithney, and there the Fair remained, with its wrestling contests, street stalls, and Leat Court in a room at the Arms. Tenants paid their rents to the Trevelyan Estate, settled disputes, and hired new labour.

The village is said to take its name from *Plen-Goyl-Sithney* – Goldsithney – which means 'the field of the fair of Sithney'. It is one of Cornwall's most ancient celebrations, for it had its origin before the Norman Conquest and is mentioned in the Domesday Book.

After a gap of half a century, it was revived in 1974 and is now held on the first Saturday in August to raise funds for the village hall, built in 1973. Almost £1,000 resulted in 1986, the secretary Mrs Molly Jago tells me.

BELOW **Cornish wrestlers in action. The sport still thrives.**

Father Time, a Queen on a white horse, six Maids in white, six boys who make an archway of elm branches, dancers, a marshall, page and flower girls who scatter petals along the Queen's path, all combine for a most delightful tradition.

The Marhamchurch Revel is still flourishing gaily. It is always held on the Monday following the Feast of St Marwenne – 12 August – the Celtic Saint who brought Christianity to the village in the sixth century, I was told by enthusiast, Mrs Gladys Cann.

The schoolchildren elect their Queen and her officers. After the procession along the road from Court Farm to the war memorial, she is crowned, on the spot where St Marwenne had her cell, by Father Time. His identity is kept a strict secret and he disappears back into the church after the crowning ceremony. He makes a speech which tells that 'down the ages I have heard the peal of merry bells from yonder ancient tower ring in the joy of Marwenne's holiday.

'Long years ago, before that fame was built and blest, your village dwelt in heathen night. Then Marwenne came and brought it heavenly light. And now each year to honour her you crown to be your yearly Queen a chosen maid who must be fair and sweet and

Marhamchurch Revel

Monday following Feast of 12 August

BELOW **A unique Cornish delight. Father Time crowns the Queen of Marhamchurch Revel.**

81

staid. That she may carry on St Marwenne's light of holy woman's influence.

'And as I pass I pray this ancient custom gay may e're be kept with greater joy and fun, and Marwenne's shining memory always find a golden place in every Saintly mind.

'Now look that this by all be Seen, I here do crown thee of this year the Queen.'

After the crowning the Queen rides a white horse around the village, followed by her retinue. The Revel has close ties with the church – there is a St Marwenne hymn – and almost everyone in the village, plus the band, joins in the happy occasion.

Harvest Festivals

SEPTEMBER & OCTOBER

BELOW RIGHT **Parson Hawker of Morwenstow, credited with introducing the harvest festival.**

O f all Cornwall's great eccentrics – and its vicars stand head and shoulders among them – Parson Hawker of Morwenstow has a place of his own. Some even believe they have seen his ghost!

His song, *Trelawny,* is Cornwall's national anthem. He came to this remote parish in 1834 and stayed for 41 years, changing the suspicion of the local people to love.

It is to this country parson that the introduction of the Harvest Festival into the church is credited. A neighbour at Launceston, the Reverend Daunt, claimed to have 'invented' it, but whoever and whatever, it has become part of the season's tapestry now.

In church and chapel, pub and school, the harvests of the sea and the field, and of the world, are enjoyed every September and October. The fish and nets, the corn and wheat and vegetables make a reassuring picture and the hymns have a special appeal.

'All is safely gathered in' is the famous line, but many a Cornish wag will rhyme it, especially after a wet summer, with 'Except ten acres down Penryn'.

FAR RIGHT **This procession at St Day is part of the Festival of Our Lady of Walsingham. Each year, on a Saturday early in September, the celebration includes Eucharist at mid-day, a picnic lunch, a guest speaker, and a procession when the Walsingham Hymn is sung. The Vicar, the Reverend Paul Foot, told me that 1987 is the 25th anniversary of an annual visit to Walsingham, from Cornwall. The 'old' church in the background is now roofless and empty.**

The final sheaf of corn at harvest time, 'the neck', gives rise to a delightful old ceremony. 'Crying the Neck' is acted out in fields throughout Cornwall. It is waved aloft by the farmer who cries, 'I Have'n, I Have'n,' and in reply to the question 'What Havee?', proclaims 'A Neck, a Neck!'

Decorated with ribbons and flowers, it was carried home – in the old days – and hung up in the kitchen. The reapers would cry, 'We Yen! We Yen!' — we have ended.

I like the old tale of the reaper running to the farmhouse with the neck, where the dairymaid stood guard with a pail of water. If he could get in unseen then he could 'lawfully' kiss her – if not he was soused.

The 'neck' was kept to ensure another good harvest, and nowadays the ceremonies often end with a church service. In many places it is woven into a Corn Dolly, an art which has been regularly exhibited in recent years.

Crying the Neck

HARVEST TIME

FAR LEFT **Mr Cyril Orchard 'Cries the Neck' at Gulval in 1984.**

LEFT '**Crying the Neck' at Tregellast Barton, St Keverne.**

RIGHT Mr Lennox Green holds high the corn at the 'Crying the Neck' ceremony in West Cornwall.

FAR RIGHT The lovely Corn Dollies on display.

Once again I ask you: Is there Peace?

That is the cry by the Grand Bard before he opens the annual Gorsedd of Cornwall on the first Saturday of September.

Some 200 blue-robed men and women, elected for their contribution to Cornish culture and spirit in all its aspects, gather for these ceremonies that began in 1928 at Boscawen Un, near Land's End, and had their Golden Jubilee in 1978. Much of it is conducted in the Cornish language; there is music and dancing; but behind all the pageantry lies a more practical significance.

Gorsedd

First Saturday in September

FAR LEFT A procession, including the initiates, towards the Merry Maidens, scene of the 1986 Gorsedd.

BELOW A view of the Gorsedd, with the author on the right.

'Its main aim lies in representing the whole spectrum of Cornish culture, every strand, from language to archaeology,' said Richard Jenkin, Grand Bard for many years, and also a former secretary and deputy Grand Bard. 'It can also act as a bridge between all who feel there is something special about Cornwall.' For these are the College of Bards, bound together by the same laws, but who each have their own special interests which they can contribute to the whole, and can share with one another.

BELOW The impressive moment near the end of the Cornish Gorsedd, with Grand Bard Richard Jenkin and Swordbearer John Chesterfield.

ABOVE **The Gorsedd at Launceston in 1947 with Grand Bard R. Morton Nance being offered the Fruits of the Earth.**

With the diamond jubilee in 1988 has come a strong international aspect, for at the Gorsedd two years earlier, four Bards from Australia were initiated. A special ceremony for the eight now 'Down Under', along lines similar to the Gorsedd Proclamation, has been prepared.

Down the years some 800 Bards have been welcomed. The Gorsedd begins with the 'Corn Gwlas', the Horn of the Nation, being sounded to the four corners of Cornwall, and is opened after the cry of Peace!

The flower dance by the schoolgirls, and the offering of the Fruits of the Earth by the Lady of Cornwall, is always a colourful and charming scene.

> *Emblem of His bounty free,*
> *Take this Offering from me,*
> *As from the Hearth of Cornwall.*

There are songs and prayers, former comrades are remembered, new Bards are initiated, and presentations made for distinguished services in many aspects of Cornish artistic and social life.

The Bards end with the promise on 'The Sword of Arthur' to be ever loyal to Cornwall, our Motherland.

Possibly the oldest and largest fair in the Cornish year is at Summercourt. It spills over on to the main A30, with over 100 stalls. After all, the Fair was there before the road was built!

It has been traced back to 1201, Kenneth Mellow tells me. It was a rendezvous for farmers to buy and sell their stock, and gave labourers a chance to look for a new boss. Known as the 'Old Fair', it is held on 25 September, unless that date falls on a Saturday or Sunday, when it takes place on the Monday.

Everything from a safety pin to bedding can be bought here, and there is plenty of entertainment for the thousands of visitors, with the showmen in the Fairfield and the stalls on the road.

The Fair rights were held by the Lord of the Manor, and the 'Charter' is privately owned today. It retains its popular atmosphere.

Summercourt Fair

25 SEPTEMBER
If a Saturday or Sunday
then the following Monday

FAR LEFT The gravity wheel provides fun at Summercourt Fair.

BELOW There is plenty of fun on the Ghost Train.

Honey Fair at Callington, on the first Wednesday in October, thrives again. The Market Charter for the town was granted by Henry III in 1267, and an annual fair appointed to be held at the festival of the nativity of the Virgin Mary. There were many bees on the Kit Hill moors, and the honey was brought for sale.

The town's Richard John Trevithick, a Cornish enthusiast, revived the Fair in 1978, and now honey competitions and an exhibition hive are combined with market stalls and a fun fair to increase the local interest, all in the centre of the town.

Honey Fair at Callington
FIRST WEDNESDAY IN OCTOBER

LEFT **A big crowd for Callington's Honey Fair.**

FAR LEFT **A prize every time at Summercourt Fair.**

Allantide

**HALLOWE'EN
31 OCTOBER**

Allantide was still a popular occasion in my Newlyn childhood, and the extra-large 'Allan Apples' very much in demand. The older girls put them under their pillows to dream of their sweethearts, while the boys hung them on a string and took large bites!

The date is Hallowe'en, 31 October, and it is all done for good luck. The girls would learn who their future husband would be ... but they could use a less uncomfortable method. In olden days three names were put on separate pieces of paper, in the centre of three balls of earth. Miss M. A. Courtney records: 'These were afterwards put into a deep basin of water, and anxiously watched until one of them opened, as the name on the first slip which came to the surface would be that of the person you were to marry.'

Allantide is also the time of one of Cornwall's enthusiastically celebrated Feasts, St Just, the nearest Sunday to 31 October.

As well as special services and parades, sporting contests and church bazaars, there is a regular and popular Monday Meet of the Western Hunt, with the town square packed. It is a great time for re-unions, because St Just lost thousands of its people through emigration to the four corners of the mining world.

> *St Just bugs, leathern jugs,*
> *Curdy milk and whey;*
> *Boil the maggots in the crock,*
> *On Allan Feasten-day.*

St Just Feast

NEAREST SUNDAY TO 31 OCTOBER

The name of Guy Fawkes may stand for treachery and failure in English history but, curiously enough, the 5 November anniversary brings more celebration than St George's Day or the Queen's birthday.

In Cornwall there are bonfires and fireworks galore, at playing fields and back gardens. It may be a worrying time for firemen – and parents – but the children revel in the excitement and thrill of danger.

While so many annual events have died out 'Remember, Remember' has come in for a big revival in our lifetime.

NOVEMBER

Guy Fawkes Day

5 NOVEMBER

ABOVE LEFT **St Just Feast Monday retains its popularity, as this Meet of the Western Hunt proves.**

LEFT **Almost every day of the week in Cornwall's hunting season there is a Meet of Foxhounds. Here, in the 1950s, the Western Hunt gathers at Rosehill, Penzance.**

One day Prince William may be the focus of one of Cornwall's most ancient and now quaint Royal ceremonies, to receive at Launceston his 'Feudal Dues'. For this would be his right as Duke of Cornwall, the eldest son of the monarch ... as his father must surely recall. It was in November 1973, just twenty years after the Coronation of the new Queen, that Prince Charles came to the Norman Castle to hear the proclamation.

Those symbolic dues, or rents, offered in token 'in recollection of days long past', now have a place of pride in the Launceston Museum, and include a grey cloak, a salmon spear, a pair of white gloves, a pound of pepper and a carriage of wood. Not on show are the greyhounds Whisky and Soda, presented that day. 'I know I'm not allowed to keep them,' the Duke quipped. In response to the gifts he gave each donor a white rod, and said: 'I hereby confirm you and those you represent, tenants, and give you and them peaceable and quiet seizin and possession of the Manors, Lands and tenancies which you hold or represent, according to ancient custom.'

It was Richard, Earl of Cornwall (1209 - 1272), the second son of King John, who confirmed the grant of Launceston as a free borough, a major Charter. He allowed the people to build a Guildhall, charging an annual 'pound of pepper'. He was also paid 100 silver shillings ... and so the 'Feudal Dues' ceremonies had their beginning.

Presentation of Feudal Dues Launceston

FAR LEFT **It was in November 1973 that Prince Charles received his Feudal Dues as Duke of Cornwall during a visit to Launceston. Here he walks through the castle with the Mayor Mr Jack Moore.**

BELOW **These young ladies of Launceston discovered that it was not all ceremony and tradition when the Prince came a-visiting.**

'Fair Mo' is still a happy memory for the old folk of St Ives, particularly the stalls around the market house and church, but today's events retain the traditional name. It means Pig Fair, for in times long past, as Cyril Noall records, pigs were kept in large numbers at the Breakwater and Porthmeor, and the meat was sold from street stalls.

Over the years it changed to become a children's feast, with macaroons and fairings, 'clidgy' and toys, and continued until the wartime blackout stopped such outdoor fun.

Mrs Beryl James, local historian and former Mayor, told me it is celebrated on the nearest Saturday to the end of November – St Andrew's Feast – with a parish church 'fair' or bazaar at the Guildhall. She believes it enjoyed such popularity in the old days because the mackerel season was in full swing, and the local folk had a little more money in their purses just before Christmas.

Fair Mo

**Nearest Saturday
to end of November**

FAR LEFT With a smile Mr Kenneth J. Uglow, the oldest tenant of the Duchy of Cornwall at that time, presents the Duke with a faggot of wood from the farm and a spear. These are two of the traditional gifts.

BELOW Fair Mo survives at St Ives, and in November 1963 the Mayor and Mayoress, Alderman and Mrs E.P. Curnow, sample the fairings.

Carol singing is as inspiring in Cornwall today as it can ever have been. Although they do not ring through the tin mines as they did in the old days when miners came to 'grass' on the man-engines, and although the church and chapel choirs are not as strong as they once were, the tradition thrives. The male voice choirs, and the combined get-togethers for this special music, sound a jubilant note.

Much of the great Christmas music is heard in the Camborne-Redruth area, where several composers had their home, and the Cornish miners took these songs around the world.

What splendid names the tunes were given: *Flaming Seraphs, Hark What Music Fills Creation, Holy Voices,* and *The Angel's Song.* It was a wave of musical Cornish expression which we still treasure.

The carols of Thomas Merritt, who died in 1908, at the age of 46, have an ever-increasing popularity. A Methodist and chapel organist at Illogan Highway his harmonies, linked to stirring verses, have a distinctive Cornish energy and enthusiasm. They have become the folk carols of Cornwall around the world.

One ancient Westcountry carol, with a full measure of dialect is worth recalling. Holy Mary says to the Child:

> *Go the Wayst out, Child Jesus,*
> *Go the Wayst out to Play;*
> *Down by God's Holy Well*
> *I saw Three pretty children*
> *As ever tongue can tell.*

Perhaps someone can set that to music.

We didn't hear so much about Christmas turkeys until more recent times. A 'commercial' 100 years ago summed up the sentiment:

> *We have seen good old customs abolished,*
> *To our anger, vexation and grief,*
> *May we ne-er grow so dainty and polished,*
> *As at Christmas to fail from roast beef.*

West Cornwall has a new dimension to its Christmas festivities with the harbour lights of Mousehole and Newlyn. These are switched on a few days before Christmas, after months of work by volunteers, and continue for a week or so after.

These are brilliant attractions not to be missed: certainly two of Cornwall's finest free shows.

FAR LEFT **Members of Four Lanes Male Voice Choir join in the Cornish carols.**

Christmas Lights

Tom Bawcock's Eve

23 DECEMBER

If there is one place in Cornwall where Christmas celebrations get underway two days early it is 'Mousehole 'pon Tom Bawcock's Eve'. That stalwart fisherman Tom, as legend would have us believe – although there are other theories – caught 'seven sorts of fish' on 23 December, enough to feed the famished village.

The song always goes down well, and so does the Starry Gazey Pie, with the fish heads poking out of the crust, which is consumed in great quantities, with many a pint of beer.

The story is sung with fervour at the Ship Inn, and the Coastguard Hotel, to the delight of locals and furriners.

To be there then who would'n wish
To sup on seven sorts of fish.

FAR LEFT AND LEFT **Tom Bawcock's celebrations at the Ship Inn, Mousehole, with Leslie Nicholls as the famous fisherman alongside the Starry-gazey pie, and landlord and landlady Michael and Tracey Maddern.**

Nativity Plays

Father Bernard Walke of St Hilary, brought national fame to his lovely church near Marazion with the 1927 radio broadcast of his nativity play *Bethlehem*. He wrote it as an act of worship for the people of the parish, played out within the church. It received not only public acclaim but also the admiration of the Prime Minister.

Today there is no nativity play at St Hilary, broadcast to the nation, but in many a Cornish church and chapel at Christmas the tender story of the birth of Jesus in the stable, and the arrival of the Wise Men and the Kings in the presence of the animals remains a precious adornment.

BELOW A scene from a Nativity Play at St Hilary, with Father Bernard Walke joined by the Shepherds.

Christmas Eve

24 DECEMBER

What about a verse for Christmas Eve in East Cornwall?

Here's to the old apple tree!
Hat's full, packs full,
Great bushel bags full!
Hurrah! And fire off the Gun.

It was tradition to take a jar of cider, a bottle and a gun to the orchard, and put a small apple bough into the bottle before reciting the verse. The people went in procession, saluted a tree and sprinkled it with cider to make sure of a good summer harvest. It is a custom that has long since disappeared, I'm assured, in this area.

They had bigger crowds to watch
the parades in earlier days but many customs still flourish, incorporating
the best of the old and the new.

Bibliography

Bygone Days in Devon and Cornwall
Mrs H. P. Whitcombe

Helston Furry Dance
J. H. Hosken

Padstow's Obby Oss
Donald Rawe

The Hobby Horse etc
T. Peter

Cornish Feasts and Folk-lore
Miss M. A. Courtney

The Book of Bodmin
James Willmott

The Book of St Ives
Cyril Noall

Trewint
Thomas Shaw

Portrait of Cornwall
Claude Berry

The Folklore of Cornwall
Tony Deane and Tony Shaw

Mount's Bay
Douglas Williams

West Cornwall in the Old Days
Douglas Williams

The Silver Ball
Ivan Rabey

Helston Flora Day
Jill Newton

The Book of Launceston
Arthur Venning

Acknowledgements

My thanks go to so many who have helped, particularly Penzance Town Council and Penlee House staff; the Morrab Library, Penzance; *The Cornishman* Newspaper and staff; *The Western Morning News;* Falmouth Art Gallery (Curator Kate Dinn) and the Town Council; T. A. Gimblett; David Green; Lionel Pooley; Reverend Tom Shaw; Beryl James; Richard Warne; Ivan Rabey; Richard Jenkin; Gladys Cann; Molly Jago; Father Michael Howard; John W. Clarke; and many other friends. My special thanks, once again, to my wife Jane, to Publisher Michael Williams, and to Brenda Duxbury.

My thanks also to the following photographers: Andrew and Paul Besley (Lelant); James Tremain (St Columb); Sam Bennetts (St Ives); Phil Monckton (Penzance); Peter Hughes (Camborne); Clifford Clemens (Bodmin); Bernard White (Newquay); C.D. Bennetts (Troon); Ray Bishop (Wadebridge); John Lyne (Launceston); Dennis Jory (Sennen); Camera Craft (Truro); Jim Bottrell (Penzance); the Richards brothers, Reg and Eddie of Penzance; the late Harry Penhaul (Penzance); the late George Ellis (Bodmin); and so many others through the years.

Other Bossiney Titles Include

WEST CORNWALL IN THE OLD DAYS
by Douglas Williams.
St Ives, Mousehole, Newlyn, Penzance, St Just, Helston and Mullion are only some of the places featured in this nostalgic book. Richly illustrated.
'This Book has something of the celebratory feel about it. Mr Williams, a Bard of the Cornish Gorsedd, has produced a thoroughly delightful volume, packed with a splendid selection of photographs that span the mid-nineteenth century to the present day . . .'
Dr James Whetter, The Cornish Banner

THE MOORS OF CORNWALL
by Michael Williams, contains 77 photographs and drawings.
  The first ever publication to incorporate the three main moorland areas of Cornwall.
'An evocative and exhilarating journey . . . will instil a desire to explore . . .'
Cornish Life

E. V. THOMPSON'S WESTCOUNTRY
A memorable journey: combination of colour and black and white photography from Bristol to Land's End.
'. . . the well-known novelist takes us on a memorable journey . . . tells us of "the style and spirit of the region, its tone and tempo."'
Western Times and Gazette

COASTLINE OF CORNWALL
by Ken Duxbury
Ken Duxbury has spent thirty years sailing the seas of Cornwall, walking its clifftops, exploring its caves and beaches, using its harbours and creeks.
'. . . has used his unique experience of his years sailing around Cornwall . . .'
Cornish Scene

WESTCOUNTRY HAUNTINGS
by Peter Underwood
'The Westcountry offers . . . just about every kind of ghostly manifestation . . .' writes Peter Underwood, president of the Ghost Club. '. . . a chilling look at hauntings from Bristol to Cornwall . . . many of the accounts appear for the first time.'
David Henderson, The Cornish Guardian

NORTH CORNWALL IN THE OLD DAYS
by Joan Rendell, 147 old photographs
These pictures and Joan Rendell's perceptive text combine to give us many facets of a nostalgic way of North Cornish life, stretching from Newquay to the Cornwall/Devon border.
'This remarkable collection of pictures is a testimony to a people, a brave and uncomplaining race.'
Pamela Leeds, The Western Evening Herald

WESTCOUNTRY MYSTERIES
Introduced by Colin Wilson, 45 photographs and old drawings.
'The Westcountry isn't just a place of beauty . . . it is also a place for some curious mysteries . . . A team of authors have joined forces to re-examine and probe various yarns from the puzzling to the tragic . . . well-written and researched.'
James Besley, Bristol Evening Post

SEA STORIES OF CORNWALL
by Ken Duxbury, 48 photographs.
'This is a tapestry of true tales', writes the author, 'by no means all of them disasters – which portray something of the spirit, the humour, the tragedy, and the enchantment, that is the lot of we who know the sea.'
'Ken is a sailor, and these stories are written with a close understanding and feel for the incidents.'
James Mildren, The Western Morning News

CASTLES OF CORNWALL
by Mary and Hal Price, 78 photographs and map.
St Catherine's Castle and Castle Dore both at Fowey, Restormel near Lostwithiel, St Mawes, Pendennis at Falmouth, St Michael's Mount, Tintagel, Launceston and Trematon near Saltash. Mary and Hal Price on this tour of Cornwall explore these nine castles.
'. . . a lavishly illustrated narrative that is both historically sound and written in a compelling and vivid style that carries the reader along from one drama to the next.'
Pamela Leeds, The Western Evening Herald

100 YEARS AROUND THE LIZARD
by Jean Stubbs. 150 old photographs.
A beautiful title, relating to a magical region of Cornwall, well illustrated, with text by the distinguished novelist living near Helston.
'. . . writes with the skills of a professional novelist, the knowledge which comes from living here, and the enthusiasm which an enquiring mind can develop.'
The Western Morning News

HISTORIC INNS OF CORNWALL
by Colin Gregory
The author, a well-known Cornish journalist, explores fifty historic inns.
'... not exactly a good drinkers guide but a look at the history of public houses. It is certanly a book which should be in every motorist's glove compartment.'

The Cornish Guardian

PEOPLE & PLACES IN CORNWALL
by Michael Williams. 60 photographs
Featuring Sir John Betjeman, Marika Hanbury Tenison, Barbara Hepworth and seven other characters, all of whom contributed richly to the Cornish scene.
'Michael Williams writes about ten very different people ... openly aware of the permanent power and attraction held for them'.

The Western Morning News

UNKNOWN BRISTOL
by Rosemary Clinch
Introduced by David Foot, this was Bossiney's first Bristol title. 'Rosemary Clinch relishes looking round the corners and under the pavement stones ...'
'... with its splendid introduction by David Foot, peeps into parts of Bristol that other books do not, and I can hardly do better than steal from David's introduction a quote from that great journalist, the late James Cameron, who declared to the editors of the many papers for which he worked, "If you want the facts, you can get 'em from Reuters. I'll look beyond the facts for you." In her own way this is exactly what Rosemary Clinch has done for Bristol ...'

Heidi Best, Somerset & Avon Life

HEALING, HARMONY & HEALTH
by Barney Camfield
Healing in its various forms, the significance of handwriting and dreams, and psycho-expansion.
'If you are tuned in to the right wavelength of new age thinking ... you won't want to put it down until you get to the last page.'

David Rose, Western Evening Herald

SECRET WESTCOUNTRY
by Hilary Wreford, Rosemary Clinch & Michael Williams
Three authors search for the facts and questions behind the stories. This is a book full of puzzles and tantalizing questions.
'... many stories of mysteries, legends and intriguing events. They range in time from pre-historic to recent years ...'

The Western

HISTORIC INNS OF DEVON
by Monica Wyatt
Monica Wyatt visits fifty famous hostelries scattered over the county.
'I found this book interesting enough to want to go and visit some of these buildings ...'

Irene Roberts, The South Hams Group of Newspapers

MYSTERIES IN THE SOMERSET LANDSCAPE
by Sally Jones
Sally Jones travels among the mysteries of Somerset, mysteries which seem an organic part of the landscape.
'... an intriguing journey through the county, each part of which has its own mysteries.'

Heidi Best, Somerset & Avon Life

AROUND ST AUSTELL BAY
by Joy Wilson
'... Joy Wilson's text is as warm and as sympathetic as the lovely old pictures, making this a book which glows with interest, a soft lamplight shedding illumination on an era dimmed by the passing years. It is a beautiful achievement, and one of the very best in the Bossiney series.'

The Western Morning News

MY CORNWALL
A personal vision of Cornwall by eleven writers living and working in the county: Daphne du Maurier, Ronald Duncan, James Turner, Angela du Maurier, Jack Clemo, Denys Val Baker, Colin Wilson, C. C. Vyvyan, Aurthur Caddick, Michael Williams and Derek Tangye with reproductions of paintings by Margo Maeckelbergh.
'An ambitious collection of chapters.'

The Times, London

PARANORMAL IN THE WESTCOUNTRY
by Michael Williams
'Michael Williams of Bossiney Books has produced another of his well illustrated books of strange goings-on ... He explores ghost hunting, healing, psychic painting, tarot cards, mediumship, psycho-expansion, astrology and more.'

Allan Tudor, Herald Express

We shall be pleased to send you our catalogue giving full details of our growing list of titles for Devon, Cornwall and Somerset and forthcoming publications.

If you have difficulty in obtaining our titles, write direct to Bossiney Books, Land's End, St Teath, Bodmin, Cornwall.